YOUR KNOWLEDGE HAS V.

- We will publish your bachelor's and
  master's thesis, essays and papers

- Your own eBook and book -
  sold worldwide in all relevant shops

- Earn money with each sale

Upload your text at www.GRIN.com
and publish for free

Patrick Spieß

Stanley Kubrick's "Full Metal Jacket". Portrayal of the Vietnam War

GRIN Verlag

Bibliografische Information der Deutschen Nationalbibliothek:

Die Deutsche Bibliothek verzeichnet diese Publikation in der Deutschen National-
bibliografie; detaillierte bibliografische Daten sind im Internet über http://dnb.d-
nb.de/ abrufbar.

Imprint:

Copyright © 2013 GRIN Verlag GmbH
Druck und Bindung: Books on Demand GmbH, Norderstedt Germany
ISBN: 978-3-656-56430-0

This book at GRIN:

http://www.grin.com/en/e-book/266468/stanley-kubrick-s-full-metal-jacket-portra-
yal-of-the-vietnam-war

GRIN - Your knowledge has value

Der GRIN Verlag publiziert seit 1998 wissenschaftliche Arbeiten von Studenten, Hochschullehrern und anderen Akademikern als eBook und gedrucktes Buch. Die Verlagswebsite www.grin.com ist die ideale Plattform zur Veröffentlichung von Hausarbeiten, Abschlussarbeiten, wissenschaftlichen Aufsätzen, Dissertationen und Fachbüchern.

Visit us on the internet:

http://www.grin.com/

http://www.facebook.com/grincom

http://www.twitter.com/grin_com

Inhaltsverzeichnis

1. Introduction

The Vietnam War was a traumatic event of the recent American history. Due to harsh criticism both at home and abroad of the American involvement in Vietnam, the film industry struggled to produce notable Vietnam War films during the conflict. Only in the late 1970s Hollywood came up with significant films that were trying to came to terms with the past. Down to the present day, the film industry has produced a number of Vietnam War films. What is special about these films is that they show a high level of diversity. In this seminar paper I will examine how the Vietnam War is portrayed in *Full Metal Jacket* and outline its context in relation with other filmic presentations of the Vietnam War. In particular, I will focus on the drafting and military drill of young men, as well as on the effects that the drill and the war itself had on recruits. I will first introduce the historical event the film is dealing with and outline its filmic presentations and film-historical context. Then I will briefly introduce the film and provide information regarding its historical context. The central question of this paper is, which specific perspective is illustrated in *Full Metal Jacket* and to what extent the film can be classified along other Vietnam War films. In resuming thoughts I will first establish what stance *Full Metal Jacket* takes towards the Vietnam War and how this perspective is created. Finally I will introduce selected scenes and examine the method of the film in portraying the Vietnam War.

2. Historical Event

2.1 Vietnam War

The Vietnam War was a part of a conflict in Indochina that has lasted for thirty years. The conflict occurred 1945 as a result of a resistance movement of the Vietnamese communists against the French colonial rule and led to a civil war between North and South Vietnam. From 1960 the United States started to support South Vietnam, firstly by dispatching military advisors and from 1965 by the massive use of their armed forces. From 1973 United States forces were gradually withdrawn and 1975 Vietnam was unified under communist rule.[1] In the following I am going to focus on the

---

1   Cf. Mark Atwood Lawrence, *The Vietnam War: A Concise International History* (Oxford: University Press, 2008).

recruitment of American soldiers, the training in the boot camps, as well as the assignment for the war in Vietnam. These are the central aspects, *Full Metal Jacket* is dealing with.

During the war period between 1964 and 1973 approximately 8,615,000 men served in the armed forces of the United States. There were two ways of entering the military: men either volunteered or were drafted. Roughly 2,215,000 men were drafted and had to serve for two years in the armed forces. All men at the age of 18 had to register for the draft. However, since the Korean War ended in 1953 and the armed forces were well filled, the military took steps to reduce the number of potential recruits to a prudent level. As a result, all men between 18 and 25 were in a primary pool. This led to an average age of 22 for a soldier fighting in Vietnam, which is very young. In comparison to World War I and II, where the average age was about 26. Theoretically, all recruits were treated equally, regardless of race or class. Practically, however, the draft fell mainly on minorities and the working class, while especially middle- and upper-class whites could avoid induction.[2]

All recruits were required to complete a basic training, which usually lasted for eight weeks. The basic training at boot camp "was as much psychological as it was physical, designed to disabuse a recruit of his civilian preconceptions and teach him to think like a soldier."[3] Boot camp training had basically three aims: firstly, to identify and eradicate their weakness; secondly, prepare them for combat in Vietnam; and, thirdly, promote coherence and fraternity among the recruits.[4] These goals are directly linked with the military strategy of the United States, namely counterinsurgency and attrition. This strategy included search and destroy missions, in which platoons were inserted into hostile territory by helicopters and were supposed to search the Viet Cong and their base areas, destroy them, and withdraw instantly. Moreover, many free-fire zones were established, in which any unidentified person was considered as an enemy, and soldiers were permitted to shoot anyone. Hence, this strategy required the production of a soldier, who would not recognise potential targets as fellow human beings, and kill anyone without hesitation.[5]

---

2 Cf. James E. Westheider, *The Vietnam War* (Westport, Connecticut: Greenwood Press, 2007), 31-107.
3 Ibid., 51.
4 Cf. Ibid.
5 Cf. Michael Klein, "Historical Memory, Film, and the Vietnam Era," in: *From Hanoi to Hollywood: The Vietnam War in American Film*, ed. Linda Dittmar and Gene Michaud (New

In order to achieve this, the drill instructor took a key role during basic training. Drill instructors "shouted at, kicked, cursed, harassed, and humiliated the recruits,"[6] so that they learned quickly to obey orders immediately without thinking. Furthermore, the military sought to promote collectivity by shaving the recruits heads and shipping all their belongings back home. Anything that could remind a recruit of his civilian life was taken away.[7] The training was both physically and psychologically hard. Recruits who performed poorly were constantly abused. Especially drill instructors had a down on underachievers. John Ketwig remembers that his drill instructor nicknamed a chubby recruit "Fatso" and abused him regularly shouting "You're fat! Fat! FAT. You're a fat, filthy, fucking pig, aren't you, boy?".[8] Drill instructors picked on poor recruits not only because of personal antipathies, but also to encourage the strong recruits to assists the ones who are struggling, and thus promote a sense of team spirit. Additionally, boot camp training sought to turn young men into marines, airmen and so forth. They were thought of the history, traditions and heroes of their service. All recruits should see each other as brothers and stand up for each other in combat.[9] James Westheider collected many memories of boot camp recruits, and generally speaking, for the majority boot camp training was a negative experience and even few recruits broke under the abuse and committed suicide.[10]

2.2 Filmic presentations and film-historical context

When talking about filmic presentations of the Vietnam War, David Willock puts forward that there is a high diversity of Vietnam War films.[11] However, he defines four major categories: firstly, the Vietnam Veteran film investigating the struggle with the reintegration of Vietnam Veterans into society. Secondly, films depicting the Vietnam War as a catalyst for violence in the United States. Thirdly, revenge films illustrating a hero who is able to succeed, whilst the entire United States army failed to do so. And finally, combat films taking place during the period of American

Brunswick: Rutegrs University Press, 1990), 30.

6 Westheider, *The Vietnam War,* 51.

7 Cf. Brandon Johnson and Robert A. Goldberg, *"Boot Camp Violence: Abuse in Vietnam War-era Basic Training," The University of Utah's Journal of Undergraduate Research* 6 (1995): 8.

8 Cf. Westheider, *The Vietnam War,* 56.

9 Cf. Johnson and Goldberg, "Boot Camp Violence," 9.

10 Cf. Westheider, *The Vietnam War,* 57.

11 Cf. David E. Whillock, "Defining the Fictive American Vietnam War Film: In Search of a Genre." *Literature/Film Quarterly* 16, no. 4 (1988): 245.

involvement in the war.[12]

During the conflict itselft only one Vietnam film of note was produced. The patriotic film *The Green Berets* was basically a war presentation in romantic western style. One of the reasons why the American film industry was reluctant to produce Vietnam War films was the dilemma of criticising the Vietnam War on the one hand, without disparaging American ideals on the other hand. In the late 1970s the film industry finally came up with a first batch of notable films like *Coming Home, The Deer Hunter* and *Apocalypse Now* that were basically emphasising the futility of the war. A third group of Vietnam War films, occurred in the early 1980s, were focusing on the veterans victimisation and revenge, for example the Rambo series. Eventually, critics outline a fourth phase of films made in the late 1980s and early 1990s including *Platoon, Full Metal Jacket, Casualties of War, Born on the Fourth of July* and *Heaven and Earth*. These films are characterised by their more realistic depiction of the war, and thus are a reaction against the earlier films that tended to mythicise and glorify American heroism.[13] The majority of films are prone to illustrate a mythic-ideological, predominantly individualised point-of-view. Often the story is driven by a personal tragedy and ends in an adolescent *bildungsroman*.[14]

With regard to the film-historical context, most Vietnam War films share common icons and conventions. The two most common icons are the M16 rifle and the Huey helicopter. These icons represent the military superiority of the United States compared with the village culture of the Vietnamese. They constantly remind the viewer of the inefficient use of technology and the fact that military superiority was not enough to assure the victory. Moreover, many films feature similar conventions. Especially in films made from the late 1970s, the futility of the involvement both politically and militarily appears as a convention. Additionally, the lack of visual contact with the enemy is one convention of many Vietnam War films. The view is often extremely limited, so that the enemy is mostly hidden and attacks from the

---

12 Cf. Ibid., 246.

13 Cg. Winfried Fluck, "The' Imperfect Past': Vietnam According to the Movies," in *The Merits of Memory. Concepts, Contexts, Debates*, ed. Hans-Jürgen Grabbe and Sabine Schindler (Heidelberg: Universitätsverlag C. Winter, 2008), 361f.

14 Cf. Tony Williams, "Narrative Patterns and Mythic Trajectories in Mid-1980s Vietnam Movies," in *Iventing Vietnam. The War in Film and Television,* ed Michael Anderegg (Philadelphia: Temple University Press, 1991), 118.

rear.[15] To what extent *Full Metal Jacket* fits into filmic presentation and the film-historical context, will be discussed later.

3. *Full Metal Jacket* and its historical context

Full Metal Jacket is a 1987 American war film directed by Stanley Kubrick. It is based on the Novel *The Short-Timers* by Gustav Hasford, who co-wrote the script together with Michael Herr. The film is neatly divided into two parts. The first part shows the drill of young recruits in a U.S. Marine Corps boot camp in North Carolina. The drill instructor prepares the young men for Vietnam through a process of brutalisation. One of the recruits goes progressively insane until he commits suicide, after having shot his drill instructor. The second part shifts to Vietnam, a ruined city during the Tet offensive. Private Joker joins the platoon of his best friend Cowboy in the middle of a deadly sniper fire. After Cowboy is killed, the platoon chases the sniper, who turns out to be a girl. She is in agony and begs Joker to kill her. After hesitating, because he had never killed before, he does it.

The historical context during the production time of *Full Metal Jacket* was characterised by extremely negative sentiments of the American public. Some of the reasons behind public opposition to the Vietnam War were the criticism of the draft and the reporting from Vietnam. The system of conscription which did not treat eligible men equally, drove much of the protest after 1965. On the other hand, the protest was directed against the dehumanised and violent drill of young recruits during their boot camp training.[16] Furthermore, the Tet offensive marked a major turning point in public's opinion about the involvement, because it proved that statements by the U.S. Government, who had been assuring the public that victory is within reach, were wrong. Thus the public became more and more critical towards American involvement in Vietnam and was in doubt about the credibility of its government. As a result, in a survey from 1988, 70 percent agreed with the statement that " The Vietnam War showed […] that U.S. officials […] cannot be trusted to give

---

15 Cf. Whillock, "Defining the Fictive American Vietnam War Film", 247.
16 Cf. David Cortright, *Peace: A History of Movements and Ideas* (New York: Cambridge University Press, 2008) 164.

reliable information to the public"[17] These sentiments of the public affected the films produced between 1975 and 1990. To what extent *Full Metal Jacket* reflects the public's concerns will be discussed after the analysis of the portrayal of the Vietnam War, which I shall examine in the following chapter.

4. Depiction of the Vietnam War in *Full Metal Jacket*

Full Metal Jacket takes a critical stance towards the drafting of young soldiers and their drill in boot camps by criticising the entire process by which patriarchal values, the extinction of everything female and infantilism are constructed and glorified. Stanley Kubrick is laying bare the military ideological machine by the eschewal of any identification with his characters. In the following, I shall illustrate how this perspective is created.

The Private Gomer Pyle represents the characteristics that the drill in the boot camp aims to eradicate. Already the name Gomer Pyle is a first pointer to Pyle's character. He is named after a television show that was 1968 at the height of its popularity and depicted the character of Private Gomer Pyle as naive and incompetent.[18] The role of Private Gomer Pyle is played by Jim Nabors, who finally came out as homosexual in 2013.[19] Although he denied anything during the production time, his alleged homosexuality was one of the dominant topics in the media. Thus the film implies that Pyle is far more effeminate than the others and even has an affection for men.[20]

Furthermore, Pyle is the personification of the infantilism in *Full Metal Jacket*. Throughout the film, he is depicted as a child, sucking several times his thumb and marching with his pants down and a thumb in his mouth. Another scene shows how Joker needs to button up Pyle's shirt. An action that a young man obviously is supposed to do himself. Pyle fails completely to adapt to the standards of male

17 Cf. Patrick Hagopian, *The Vietnam War in American Memory: Veterans, Memorials, and the politics of healing* (Amherest: University of Massachusetts, 2009), 25.

18 Cf. Susan White, "Male Bonding, Hollywood Orientalism, and the Repression of the Feminine in Kubrick's *Full Metal Jacket*," in *Iventing Vietnam. The War in Film and Television,* ed. Michael Anderegg (Philadelphia: Temple University Press, 1991), 207.

19 Cf. Justin Ravitz, "Jim Nabors, Gomer Pyle Star, Is Gay, Marries Partner of 38 Years," *Us Weekly*, January 30, 2013, http://www.usmagazine.com/celebrity-news/news/jim-nabors-gomer-pyle-star-is-gay-marries-partner-of-38-years-2013301 (accessed March 24, 2013).

20 Cf. White, "Male Bonding," 207.

behaviour as requested by Hartman. It is the childish nature, symbolised by Pyle, that is preventing the entire unit from moving on. During their training the marines are running through a lake of mud while Pyle falls and the whole group stumbles. Due to his infantilism, Pyle is becoming a burden to the group and thus infantilism needs to be eradicated to achieve the desirable collective identity.[21]

Angered by Pyle's mistakes for which the entire group has to carry the can, he is held down and beaten up violently with bars of soap by his comrades. Although from this point he gradually begins to fit into the group, this victimisation transforms him into a monster. Spurred on by Hartman, who glorifies Lee Harvey Oswald and Charles Whitman for their assassinations, Pyle turns the weapon on the Sargent and himself, finally shooting both dead declaring "I am in a world of shit". Despite the fact that had graduated from boot camp, Pyle is unable to deal with his own infantilism, the violence and desire for male affection, because the ideology requests to externalise this onto women and the enemy.[22]

Moreover, the boot camp part is a harsh criticism of the Marine Corps culture, because it "dehumanizes its men and reshapes them into desensitized killing machines who lack a strong individual identity once they go through basic training".[23] During their eight-week training in the boot camp on Parris Island, the recruits are audibly and visually depicted as a unit. The camera avoids to picture the privates individually. During their lineups, the men stand in the edge of the frame and respond with a collective voice, while Hartman is the dominant figure in the centre. In addition, the recruits are overcoming the obstacle in pairs, climbing the ropes and ladders together. Their movements seem to be parallel to each other and Kubrick emphases the force into a collective identity by showing the men against the background of a sunset, where they become faceless silhouettes.[24]

Furthermore, there are several other indicators that the Marine Corps try to wipe out any personality and force the young men into a collective group. First of all, the privates are all renamed. Although we see the real name of Private Joker, he is never approached by his real name. During a training exercise, Pyle fails to separate

---

21 Cf. Ibid., 206ff.
22 Cf. Ibid., 209.
23 Zivah Perel, "Pyle and Joker's Dual Narratives: Individuality and Group Identity in Stanley Kubrick's Marine Corps." *Literature/Film Quarterly* 36, no. 3 (2008): 223.
24 Cf. Ibid., 224.

between his right and left shoulder. "You did that on purpose. You want to be different!", Hartman accuses Pyle and slaps him repeatedly in the face. In one the many chanting scene the privates repeats Hartman's words "I love working for Uncle Sam/ Let me know just who I am". Kubrick criticises "the sadistic and dehumanizing process of training that strips young men of their identities and shapes them into robotlike killing machines"[25] Thus another reason why Pyle's takes both Hartman's and his own life, is that he fails "to separate his own identity from the one dictated to him by his drill instructor."[26] To sum up one can say that Kubrick creates the critical stance of the Marine Corps culture by illustrating how it destroys individual differences in order to achieve the patriarchal plurality of comradeship where every Marine is a brother and would risk his own life in order to help the platoon.

At the very beginning the drill instructor, Sergeant Hartman, announces that the recruits "are the lowest form of life on Earth" and not even "human beings" until they finish the boot camp. In the further course Hartman addresses the soldiers as "ladies", "queers", "fags" and "sailors", "using the female label as a sign of contempt until they qualify, at which point they are suddenly told they are brothers."[27] Consequently, the entire femininity is then systematically eradicated and replaced with "weapon". Hartman forces the recruits to give their rifle a girl's name and sleep with them every night, because this is the "only pussy" they are going to get. Furthermore, this is also illustrated by the recruits chanting "I don't want no teenage queen/ I just want my M-14". However, Kubrick never attempts to divide the soldier from sex, it is only the "female" part of the sexuality, romance and love, that needs to be eradicated. On the contrary, Kubrick uses sexuality to reinforce patriarchal constructions of masculinity and femininity in society. During the second half of the film in Vietnam occur two hooker scenes. In both scenes the soldiers are negotiating with the hookers about the price, which promotes the strength and power of the man economic viability of the women. In the second hooker scene occurs a dispute about who is taking the hooker first. Private Eightball warns Private Animal Mother not to "get between a dog and his meat", however, Animal Mother gains the upper hand and

---

25 Klein, "Historical Memory, Film, and the Vietnam Era," 30.
26 Perel, "Pyle and Joker's Dual Narratives," 226.
27 Michael Pursell, "Full Metal Jacket: The Unravelling of Patriarchy." *Literature/Film Quarterly* 16, no. 4 (1988): 221.

takes the hooker first. This demonstrates that sexuality is reduced to a need and women are just a means to an end.[28] George Gilder aptly puts it:

> "The good things are manly and collective; the despicable are feminine and individual, (...) when you want to create a group of male killers, that is what you do, you kill the women in them. That is the lesson of the Marines."[29]

That is exactly the process *Full Metal Jacket* is illustrating. Kubrick critically reflects the construction of a masculine identity by wiping out anything infantile and female.

The part of the film taking place in Vietnam is about putting their gained skills into practice. Kubrick shows several men, who represent the perfect killer, according to the Marine Corps ideology. When Joker and Rafterman are being flown into battle, a machine-gunner fires at innocent civilians. Joker asks: "How can you shoot women, children...". The machine-gunner answers: "Easy - you just don't lead them so much". Joker's question implies the dehumanising ideology of the Marine Crops, which systematically attempts to eradicate all traces of feminism and infantilism.[30]

Another crucial character is Animal Mother, "the most competent, the most brutal and dehumanized, who is the perfect survival machine; Animal equals 'pure existence,' embodying the condition forced on all combat soldiers in wartime."[31] Animal Mother represents the ideal type of a soldier and the Marine Corps seeks to force all recruits into this stage. He demonstrates his position of power by taking first honours with the hooker, displacing Eightball. Moreover, he is the one, who risks his life and attempts to rescue his comrades when two of them are wounded by the sniper. He is driven by in the name of fraternity, which was established during the boot camp training. The phrase "I became death" is written on Animal Mothers helmet. This implies that his feminine and infantile side is already dead and he has become a perfect killer machine.[32] As well other men in the platoon represents bestiality and viciousness. Crazy Earl introduces his "bro", who is a dead Viet Cong

---

28 Cf. Claude J Smith, Jr, "Full Metal Jacket and the Beast Within." *Literature/Film Quarterly* 16, no. 4 (1988): 229.

29 George F. Gilder, *Sexual Suicide* (New York: Quadrangle Books, 1973), 258f.

30 Cf. Klein, "Historical Memory, Film, and the Vietnam Era," 30.

31 Gerri Reaves, "From Hasford's the Short-Timers to Kubrick's Full Metal Jacket: The Fracturing of Identification." *Literature/Film Quarterly* 16, no. 4 (1988): 234.

32 Cf. White, "Male Bonding," 211.

and allegedly has birthday. He talks sarcastically very positive about the Vietnamese, because there will not be anyone, who is "worth killing" when they return home.[33] So Kubrick is arguing that war is an instrument to manufacture patriarchal values through a process of selection. Its survivors are those, who eradicated everything that oppose masculinity and thus are resurrected and reborn as symbols of the patriarchal society.

Throughout the Vietnam section we notice that Joker is hardly involved in any combat. Although he fires at NVA soldiers from distance, he never confronts the enemy face to face. What is also apparent is the inner conflict of Joker by the contrast between the peace symbol on his uniform and the "Born to Kill" slogan on his helmet. In the second of two scenes where Joker is asked about this contrast, he replies that he is "trying to suggest something about the duality of man [...] the Jungian thing". This implies that Joker has not become a perfect killer yet, because there is still humanity inside of him.[34] As co-writer Michael Herr registers, Kubrick took up the Jungian theory deliberately, because he asked whether Herr had read any Jung and was familiar with the concept of the shadow, the dark side.[35] In Jungian theory, the shadow is a part of the unconscious mind that consists of repressed weaknesses.[36] For a marine, this weakness is connected with anything infantile or feminine. As such, Full Metal Jacket illustrates what needs to be conquered in order to achieve the perfect killer, namely wiping out all humanity out of the young men. As well the split between Parris Island and Vietnam can be referred to the Jungian duality of outside and inside. In order to win the war in Vietnam, it is inevitable to win the war against itself in the Boot camp.

Joker's duality is depicted until the almost end of the film. The final act, where the platoon defeats the sniper is a crucial moment. Joker faces the enemy for the first time and is forced to recognise its humanity. To his surprise the sniper is a young Vietnamese girl. Joker's killing the sniper is not only another act of rejecting femininity and infantilism, but a suicide act. When he executes the sniper, the peace

33 Cf. Claude J, "Full Metal Jacket and the Beast Within," 229.
34 Cf. Patricia Gruben, "Practical Joker: The Invention of a Protagonist in Full Metal Jacket." *Literature/Film Quarterly* 33, no. 4 (2005): 274.
35 Cf. Micheal Herr, *Kubrick* (New York: Grove Publishing, 2000), 6.
36 Cf. Perel, "Pyle and Joker's Dual Narratives," 228.

button on his chest disappears from view and only the slogan "Born to Kill" remains. By killing his humanity, Joker becomes another war zombie like Animal Mother. Exactly this type of soldiers the war machine is seeking to create.[37]

In summary, it can be stated that *Full Metal Jacket* takes a critical stance towards the drafting of young men and their dehumanised drill in armed forces. Kubrick demonstrates how war strips the individual identities of young men and forges them into killing machines by reinforcing patriarchal values. One can even go further and assert that *Full Metal Jacket* is not primarily about the Vietnam War, but about the war machine itself. Kubrick lays bare that patriarchal qualities are not inherent, but socially constructed. *Full Metal Jacket* criticises the process of this constructed patriarchal ideology that ultimately requires the eradication of the very self, so that its survivors are symbols of the manufactured masculine society. Kubrick achieves this perspective by avoiding any sympathy and identification with the character. In the following chapter I will discuss these methods in detail.

5. Methodical Analysis of scenes

As briefly outlined above, Kubrick uses techniques to distance the viewer from the characters. Although Joker is the character who recurs most often and provides the voice-over, he presents just a possible point of view, rather than being a guide for the viewer. In the first part Jokers voice-over is reduced to a minimum. There are seven brief utterances and the first one occurs only after seven minutes. Almost until the end of the boot camp Joker appears as a minor part, while the story is driven by the dehumanisation of Pyle. The reduced voice-over creates the impression of a distant observation of the act, rather than a subjective, personal view through a character.[38]

In the further course of the film, Kubrick continues to avoid any identification with his characters. Instead, he is offering a roaming identification through the panoramic point-of-view technique. The method of achieving this panoramic perspective becomes evident in the graveside scene. The viewer is placed in the grave with the dead soldier through a subjective camera shot, and in turn, each

---

37 Cf. Pursell, "Full Metal Jacket: The Unravelling of Patriarchy," 223.
38 Cf. Gruben, "Practical Joker," 273.

soldier offers his philosophy, ranging from that the soldiers had die "for a good cause" to "better you than me".[39] We see how each soldier is looking directly at the viewer. Each marine is given about the same time to express his opinion about the soldiers killed in action and thus Kubrick forces to viewer think about his on philosophy, instead of just illustrate an approach through one main character.

Another crucial scene is when the marines are interviewed by a documentary crew. Each soldier is condensed to a concise ideological function: Animal Mother thinks only in military objectives, Cowboy points out that the Vietnam War is what he "thought a war was supposed to be", Rafterman is completely naïve and keen on combat. Crazy Earl does not know whether America belongs to Vietnam, but he definitely belongs to Vietnam. Doc Jay believes that should not have interfered in the conflict and the Vietnamese need to care for themselves. Eightball sees death as freedom, stating "they'd rather be alive than free". Finally, Joker concludes the scene commenting "I wanted to see exotic Vietnam, the jewel of Southeast Asia. I wanted to meet interesting and stimulating people of an ancient culture and kill them".[40] Again, Kubrick offers various opinions and distances the audience from Joker through his inappropriate comment. Additionally, at the beginning of the sniper scene, Kubrick uses a subjective shot once again showing the snipers point-of-view. With that one subjective shot Kubrick detaches the viewer's identification from the group.[41] As these examples illustrate, Kubrick fractures identification throughout the film, so that

> "panoramic identification techniques result, paradoxically, in the spectator's achieving no permanent identification; instead, we migrate from one character to another, our identification repeatedly undercut. Kubrick never allows us to consider Joker as anything approximating a hero."[42]

It is exactly this fracturing of identification that distances the viewer from the characters and avoids any sympathy to them. Thus, unlike many other Vietnam War films, *Full Metal Jacket* is far from being a film about a hero or a story told from the point of view of a main character. It is rather a film about how war shapes young

---

39 Cf. Reaves, "From Hasford's the Short-Timers to Kubrick's Full Metal Jacket," 234.
40 Cf. Ibid.
41 Cf. Ibid., 235.
42 Ibid.

men into killing machines. Regarding film conventions of the period, *Full Metal Jacket* falls in line other films by frequently showing M16 rifles and Huey helicopters. In addition the film follows the convention of the lack visual contact with the enemy. In the only scene where the enemy is humanised, the sniper is hidden and the view for the platoon is extremely limited. Furthermore, *Full Metal Jacket* reflects the nations attitude towards Vietnam. Especially the first part of the film depicts the concerns about futility of the war that deprives young men of their life and shapes young men. The second part illustrates the work of military journalism that was extremely distorted. Journalists were forced to distort the truth to counteract negative image of the war in the United States.

6. Conclusion

In this seminar paper I have illustrated that Full Metal Jacket provides a critical statement of military drill of young men and unmasks the real intentions of the war machine. It became clear how war reinforces patriarchal values including the eradication of anything female and infantile to create a perfect killer. By avoiding of a heroisation of his characters, Kubrick illustrates that war is always manufactured and lays bare the ideology of the military machine that steals adolescent life away, and replaces it with one constructed man-made ideology.

Unlike many other Vietnam War films, *Full Metal Jacket* presents a more realistic view on the Vietnam War. Kubrick does not try to find an answer to the question whether the war was right or wrong. Nor he is sending his main character to search for the truth. Instead he forces the viewer to form his own opinion on the American involvement in Vietnam by reflecting the event as neutral as possible.

Bibliography

Cortright, David. *Peace: A History of Movements and Ideas.* New York: Cambridge University Press, 2008.

Fluck, Winfried. "The' Imperfect Past': Vietnam According to the Movies," in *The Merits of Memory. Concepts, Contexts, Debates*, ed. Hans-Jürgen Grabbe and Sabine Schindler 353-385. Heidelberg: Universitätsverlag C. Winter, 2008.

Gilder, George F. *Sexual Suicide.* New York: Quadrangle Books, 1973.

Gruben, Patricia. "Practical Joker: The Invention of a Protagonist in Full Metal Jacket." *Literature/Film Quarterly* 33, no. 4 (2005): 270-279.

Hagopian, Patrick. *The Vietnam War in American Memory: Veterans, Memorials, and the politics of healing.* Amherest: University of Massachusetts, 2009.

Herr, Micheal. *Kubrick.* New York: Grove Publishing, 2000.

Johnson, Brandon and Goldberg, Robert A. "Boot Camp Violence: Abuse in Vietnam War-era Basic Training," *The University of Utah's Journal of Undergraduate Research* 6 (1995): 7-15.

Klein, Michael. "Historical Memory, Film, and the Vietnam Era," in: *From Hanoi to Hollywood: The Vietnam War in American Film*, ed. Linda Dittmar and Gene Michaud, 19-41. New Brunswick: Rutegrs University Press, 1990.

Lawrence, Mark Atwood. *The Vietnam War: A Concise International History.* Oxford: University Press, 2008.

Perel, Zivah. "Pyle and Joker's Dual Narratives: Individuality and Group Identity in Stanley Kubrick's Marine Corps." *Literature/Film Quarterly* 36, no. 3 (2008): 223-233.

Pursell, Micheal. "Full Metal Jacket: The Unravelling of Patriarchy." *Literature/Film Quarterly* 16, no. 4 (1988): 218-225.

Ravitz, Justin. "Jim Nabors, Gomer Pyle Star, Is Gay, Marries Partner of 38 Years," *Us Weekly*, January 30, 2013, http://www.usmagazine.com/celebrity-news/news/jim-nabors-gomer-pyle-star-is-gay-marries-partner-of-38-years-2013301 (accessed March 24, 2013).

Reaves, Gerri. "From Hasford's the Short-Timers to Kubrick's Full Metal Jacket: The Fracturing of Identification." *Literature/Film Quarterly* 16, no. 4 (1988): 232-237.

Smith, Claude J Jr. "Full Metal Jacket and the Beast Within." *Literature/Film Quarterly* 16, no. 4 (1988): 226-231.

Westheider, James E. *The Vietnam War.* Westport, Connecticut: Greenwood Press, 2007.

Whillock, David E. "Defining the Fictive American Vietnam War Film: In Search of a Genre." *Literature/Film Quarterly* 16, no. 4 (1988): 244-250.

White, Susan. "Male Bonding, Hollywood Orientalism, and the Repression of the Feminine in Kubrick's *Full Metal Jacket*," in *Iventing Vietnam. The War in Film and Television,* ed. Michael Anderegg, 204-237. Philadelphia: Temple University Press, 1991.

Williams, Tony. "Narrative Patterns and Mythic Trajectories in Mid-1980s Vietnam Movies," in *Iventing Vietnam. The War in Film and Television,* ed. Michael Anderegg, 114-140. Philadelphia: Temple University Press, 1991.

Lightning Source UK Ltd.
Milton Keynes UK
UKIC02n1326021115
261922UK00005B/26